AAT

Cash and Financial Management

Pocket Notes

These Pocket Notes support study for the following AAT qualifications:
AAT Diploma in Professional Accounting – Level 4
AAT Diploma in Business Skills – Level 4
AAT Diploma in Professional Accounting at SCQF Level 8

British library cataloguing-in-publication data

A catalogue record for this book is available from the British Library.

Published by:
Kaplan Publishing UK
Unit 2 The Business Centre
Molly Millars Lane
Wokingham
Berkshire
RG41 2QZ

ISBN 978-1-83996-086-4

© Kaplan Financial Limited, 2021

Printed and bound in Great Britain.

CONTENTS

Preface

These Pocket Notes contain the key things that you need to know for the exam, presented in a unique visual way that makes revision easy and effective.

Written by experienced lecturers and authors, these Pocket Notes break down content into manageable chunks to maximise your concentration.

Quality and accuracy are of the utmost importance to us so if you spot an error in any of our products, please send an email to mykaplanreporting@kaplan.com with full details, or follow the link to the feedback form in MyKaplan.

Our Quality Co-ordinator will work with our technical team to verify the error and take action to ensure it is corrected in future editions.

A guide to the assessment

The assessment

Cash and Financial Management (CSFT) is an optional unit in the Level 4 Diploma in Professional Accounting qualification.

Examination

CTRM is assessed by means of a computer based assessment. The CBA will last for 2 hours and consist of 8 tasks, some of which will require full written responses.

In any one assessment, students may not be assessed on all content, or on the full depth or breadth of a piece of content. The content assessed may change over time to ensure validity of assessment, but all assessment criteria will be tested over time.

Learning outcomes & weighting

1.	Prepare forecasts for cash receipts and payments	15%
2.	Prepare cash budgets and monitor cash flows	25%
3.	Understand the importance of managing finance and liquidity	15%
4.	Understand ways of raising finance and investing funds	20%
5.	Understand regulations and organisational policies that influence decisions in managing cash and finance.	25%
	Total	100%

Pass mark

To pass a unit assessment, students need to achieve a mark of 70% or more.

1

Cash and profit

- Types of cash flow.
- Cash flow and profit.
- Calculating cash flows.
- Alternative method of calculation.
- Reconciling profit to cash flows.

Types of cash flow

Cash inflows	Cash outflows

Revenue receipts
- cash sales
- receipts from credit customers

Capital receipts
- taking out a loan
- issue of more shares
- sale of non-current assets

Revenue payments
- cash purchases
- payments to credit suppliers
- wage payments
- payment of bills/expenses

Capital payments
- repayment of loans
- purchase of non-current assets

Other payments
- dividends/loan interest/ drawings

Cash flow and profit

Non-cash expenses
- profit charged with depreciation/ provisions
- no cash flow

Accruals concept
- profit calculated using accruals concept
- cash flow is actual cash flows

Cash flow v Profit

Purchase of non-current assets
- cash outflow
- profit only charged with depreciation

Sale of non-current assets
- cash inflow from proceeds
- only profit/loss on disposal included in profit
- watch out or revaluations and leases

Financing transactions
- loans/share issues are large cash inflows
- no effect on profit

Calculating cash flows

Adjust statement of profit or loss figures to calculate cash flows in a period including:

- Actual cash received from receivables
- Actual cash paid to payables
- Actual cash paid for other expenses
- Actual cash received/paid for sale/ purchase of non-current assets

Definition

- Accrual – expense incurred in a period that has not yet been paid.
- Prepayment – payment made for an expense yet to be incurred.

Example

The statement of profit or loss for C Lad's business for the quarter ended September is as follows:

	£	£
Revenue		352,000
Less: Purchases		(78,695)
		————
Gross profit		273,305
Less: Expenses		
Wages	60,560	
Rent of office	40,000	
Insurance of machinery	30,000	
Electricity	12,000	
Depreciation	3,000	
	————	
		(145,560)
Profit		127,745
		————

Extracts from the Statement of Financial Position at 1 July and 30 September show the following:

	1 July £	30 Sept £
Trade receivables	42,256	37,258
Trade payables	12,874	12,321
Accruals – Electricity	650	550
Prepayments – Rent of office	3,000	6,000

Calculate the actual business cash receipts and cash payments for the quarter to 30 September

	£
Sales receipts	356,998
Purchases	79,248
Wages	60,560
Rent of office	43,000
Insurance of machinery	30,000
Electricity	12,100
Depreciation	0

Trade receivables

Opening balance	42,256	Cash received	356,998
Sales	352,000	Closing balance	37,258
	394,256		394,256

Trade payables

Cash paid	79,248	Opening balance	12,874
Closing balance	12,321	Purchases	78,695
	91,569		91,569

Rent of Office

Opening prepayment	3,000	Income statement	40,000
Cash paid	43,000	Closing prepayment	6,000
	46,000		46,000

Electricity

Cash paid	12,100	Opening accrual	650
Closing accrual	550	Income statement	12,000
	12,650		12,650

An opening prepayment has already been paid but the closing prepayment will be paid in this period (Rent). An opening accrual will be paid in the this period whereas the closing accrual will not (Electricity).

Alternative method of calculation

Instead of using T-accounts, equations can be used to calculate the cash flows:

- Cash from receivables = opening receivables + (credit) sales - closing receivables

- Cash paid to payables = opening payables + purchases - closing payables

- Cash paid for expenses = opening accrual - opening prepayments + expense - closing accrual + closing prepayment

- Cash received on disposal of NCA = Carry value of disposed asset + gain on disposal (or - loss on disposal)

- Cash paid for additions = Change in carry value of NCA + depreciation expense.

Reconciling profit to cash flows

Reconciling profit to cash flow involves adjusting profit for the effect of cash inflows, cash outflows and non-cash items to calculate the net cash flow for the period:

- cash inflows will be added to profit
- cash outflows will be deducted from profit
- non-cash items will be added to profit

Items added to profit to calculate cash:

- depreciation (a non-cash item)
- loss on disposal (a non-cash item)
- a decrease in the receivables balance
- a decrease in the inventory balance
- an increase in the payables balance
- any excess of the tax and or interest SoPL charge over the cash paid

Items deducted from profit to calculate cash:

- profit on disposal (a non-cash item)
- an increase in the receivables balance is deducted from profit
- an increase in the inventory balance
- a decrease in the payables balance
- any excess of the cash paid for tax and or interest over the SoPL charge

2

Forecasting cash flows

- Time series analysis.
- Quantity increases and inflation.
- Regression analysis.
- Index numbers.
- Mark-ups and margins.

Time series analysis

- a set of values (for example sales volume or total sales value) that varies with time
- isolate trend using moving averages
- calculate seasonal variations
- forecast future sales levels with time series.

Example

You have been given the sales values for June to December.

Month	SalesValue (000s)
June	851
July	771
August	916
September	935
October	855
November	1000
December	1019

Step 1 – find the 3 month moving total and the trend.

Add up the first 3 items of data to find the total i.e. 851 + 771 + 916 = 2,538; then find the average of this (the trend) by dividing by three 2,538 / 3 = 846

Move down one data item from the top and repeat the process until there are no more sets of 3 data items i.e. 771 + 916 + 935 = 2,622 and divide 2,622 / 3 = 874

Month	SalesValue (000s)	3 month moving total	Trend
June	851		
July	771	2538	846
August	916	2622	874
September	935	2706	902
October	855	2790	930
November	1000	2874	958
December	1019		

Step 2 – find the seasonal variation

Once the trend has been calculated, it is possible to calculate the seasonal variation from the trend. This is how much the actual data varies from the trend. This can calculated using the additive model or the multiplicative model.

Additive model

The additive model calculates absolute numbers. The additive model calculates the absolute difference between the actual data and the trend.

Month	SalesValue (000s)	Trend	Seasonal Variation
June	851		
July	771	846	-75
August	916	874	42
September	935	902	33
October	855	930	-75
November	1000	958	42
December	1019		

Multiplicative model

The multiplicative model calculates relative numbers (percentages). The multiplicative model calculates the percentage change from the trend.

Step 3 – Predicting future cash budgets

We can plot a graph of the data to enable us to extrapolate the trend line for the next 6 to 12 months and then apply season variation data to this trend to predict future sales.

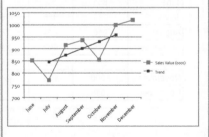

This can also been done via calculations.

The trend increases by 28 each month so 28 is added to the trend for the next months.

The seasonal variation is cyclical 42, 33, –75, 42, 33, –75 so this cycle is continued.

The sales figure equals the trend plus the seasonal variation
(A = T + V)

Month	Trend	Seasonal Variation	SalesValue (000s)
June			851
July	846	−75	771
August	874	42	916
September	902	33	935
October	930	−75	855
November	958	42	1000
December	986	33	1019
January	1014	−75	939
February	1042	42	1084
March	1070	33	1103

Quantity increases and inflation

e.g Example

Quantity increases

Sales for the final quarter of 20X5 were 100,000 units. It is anticipated that they will increase by 2% per quarter for the foreseeable future.

What is the sales quantity for each quarter of 20X6?

Solution

```
20X6 Q1 100,000 x 1.02          = 102,000 units
20X6 Q2 100,000 x 1.02 x 1.02   = 104,040 units
20X6 Q3 100,000 x 1.02 x 1.02
                        x 1.02   = 106,121 units
20X6 Q4 100,000 x 1.02 x 1.02
                 x 1.02 x 1.02   = 108,243 units
```

Inflation

Current selling price is £2 per unit. Expected to increase at the start of Q3 by 5%.

What is the sales value for each quarter of 20X6?

Solution

20X6	Q1	102,000 units x £2	= £204,000
20X6	Q2	104,040 units x £2	= £208,080
20X6	Q3	106,121 units x £2 x 1.05	= £222,854
20X6	Q4	108,243 units x £2 x 1.05	= £227,310

CBA focus

In the exam, when preparing a cash budget, you may have to use forecast information such as time series analysis to find figures for sales/purchases etc and also to be able to deal with quantity and price increases.

Regression analysis

Regression analysis is concerned with establishing the relationship between two variables.

The general equation for the regression line is given as:

$y = a + bx$

Where:

x is the independent variable

y is the dependent variable

a is the intercept on the y axis

b is the gradient of the line

You will be required to use the regression equation to forecast future values. When the regression equation is used for time series data the time periods are changed to numbers rather than specified days, months or years.

Index numbers

Index numbers can also be used to calculate a change in quantity or price.

Calculating an index number

An index number is calculated as

$$\frac{\text{Current costs}}{\text{Base costs}} \times \text{base index (usually 100)}$$

Example

With May as the base year:

Month	Cost	Calculation	Index
	£000		
May	138	138/138 × 100	100.0
June	149	149/138 × 100	108.0
July	158	158/138 × 100	114.5
August	130	130/138 × 100	94.2
Sept	136	136/138 × 100	98.6

Using an index number

Index numbers can also be used to forecast future data to be in cash flows.

The formula for using an index is

$$\frac{\text{Current index}}{\text{Base index}} \times \text{base cost}$$

Example

The current sales price of £20 was set when the index number was 100. The index numbers for the coming months are:

January 102.7

February 105.5

March 108.3

Calculate the sales prices:

January = £20 × 102.7/100 = £20.54

February = £20 × 105.5/100 = £21.10

March = £20 × 108.3/100 = £21.66

An index is a useful method of comparing figures over time by simplifying them to a single index figure that can be compared to a base year which is given an index of 100.

Mark-ups and margins

The production costs (cost of sales) may be forecast based on a predicted sales value using either a mark-up or margin basis.

Mark-up

A mark-up is a percentage added to the cost of sales to calculate the selling price. The following proforma can help you calculate3 the sales prices from the cost of sales (or vice versa) when using a mark-up.

	£	%
Sales	X	100 + mark-up
Cost of sales	(X)	(100)
Gross profit	X	Mark-up

Margin

A margin shows in percentage terms the amount of profit generated from sales i.e. what percentage of the sales revenue eventually ends up as gross profit. The following proforma can help you work back from the sales price to calculate the cost of sales using a margin.

	£	%
Sales	X	100
Cost of sales	(X)	(100 − margin)
Gross profit	X	Margin

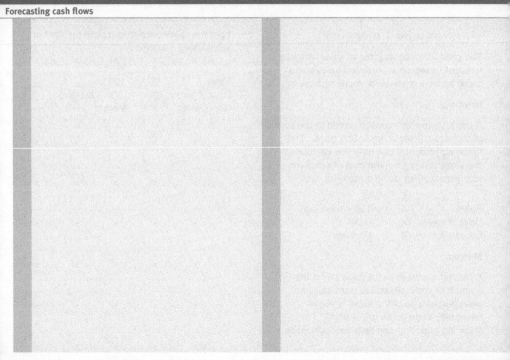

3

Preparing cash budgets

- Preparing cash budgets.
- Receipts.
- Payments.
- Exchange rates.
- Interest.
- Loans.

Preparing cash budgets

Proforma

	Jan £	Feb £	Mar £	April £	May £	June £
Receipts						
Cash sales						
Cash from receivables						
Sale of non-current assets						
Capital introduced						
Payments						
Cash purchases						
Cash to payables						
Wages						
Expenses						
Purchase of non-current assets						
Tax payments						
Net cash flow	X	X	X	X	X	X
Opening balance	X	X	X	X	X	X
Closing balance	X	X	X	X	X	X

Receipts

Sales are often made on credit and customers do not pay until subsequent periods.

The cash budget needs to show when the actual cash is expected to be received from customers, rather than the sales made.

It will be necessary to use actual and forecast sales revenue and adjust it for the effects of lagging.

Lagging of receipts affects a business's cash inflow as it will not match the sales revenue shown in the financial accounts.

Closing receivables

When calculating the cash receipts for a period, the closing receivable balance can also be forecast to be included in the financial statements.

Opening receivables

The closing receivables balance for one period becomes the opening receivables balance for the next period. When calculating the cash receipts from an opening balance, care must be taken to account for the proportion of cash that has already been received in prior months.

Example

Claude Limited sold 3,000 units of a product in June 20X3 at a selling price of £50 each. This price will increase to £55 with effect from 1 July 20X3 and this is expected to reduce demand for July to 2,800 units. Thereafter demand is expected to increase by 10% per month.

All sales are on credit and receivables pay as follows:

10% in the month of sale

50% in the month after sale

40% two months after sale and the forecast closing receivable balance at the end of August

Opening receivables for June 20X3 were:

Balance from April £58,000

Balance from May £132,750

What are the budgeted cash receipts in June, July and August 20X3 and the forecast closing receivable balance at the end of August 20X3?

	June	July	August
	£	£	£
Sales units	3,000	2,800	3,080
Selling price per unit	50	55	55
Sales	150,000	154,000	169,400
Cash receipts:			
10% in month of sale	15,000	15,400	16,940
50% in month after sale	**73,750	75,000	77,000
40% 2 months after sale	*58,000	***59,000	60,000
Total cash receipts	146,750	149,400	153,940

Notes

*All of April's outstanding balance will be received in June

**50/90 × May's outstanding balance will be received in June

***40/90 × May's outstanding balance will be received in July

Closing receivables at the end of August will consist of:

40% of Julys balance = 154,000 × 40% = £61,600

90% of Augusts balance = 169,400 × 90% = £152,460

Total closing receivables = £214,060

Payments

A business will incur expenditure when running a business, for example:

- raw materials need to be purchased
- employees need a wage
- overheads, such as rent, will be incurred

Some of the payments for these will be made in the month the cost is incurred, others will be lagged payments. Lagged payments are calculated in the same way as lagged receipts.

Closing payables

When calculating the cash payments for a period, the closing payables balance can also be forecast to be included in the statement of financial position.

Opening payables

The closing payables balance for one period becomes the opening payables balance for the next period. When calculating the cash payments from an opening balance, care must be taken to account for the proportion of cash that has already been paid in prior months.

Example

A business estimates that its credit purchases for February and March will be £16,000 but will increase by 10% each month thereafter. Its payment pattern to payables is that 40% are paid in the month after the purchases and the remaining 60% two months after the purchase.

What are the payments to payables for March, April and May and the closing payables at the end of May?

	Feb	Mar	April	May
	£	£	£	£
Purchases	16,000	16,000	17,600	19,360
Payments to payables				
One month after purchase (40%)		6,400	6,400	7,040
Two months after purchase (60%)			9,600	9,600
Cash payments		6,400	16,000	16,640

The closing payables balance as at 31st May is £29,920. This is made up of 60% of April's and 100% of May's credit sales.

Labour costs

Labour costs are normally paid in the month in which they are incurred. Labour cost can be calculated based on units produced (piecework), standard hours worked and/or an annual salary. Overtime payments/premiums may also be included in labour costs.

Example

The production budget for a company shows the following monthly production:

	April	May	June
Production (units)	6,000	6,500	7,000

Each unit of production requires three labour hours. The wage rate is £9.00 per hour for April and May increasing to £9.50 per hour in June. Normal working hours are 17,000 hours after that overtime is paid at time and a half. Overtime hours are paid in the following month.

Calculate the labour cost for inclusion in the cash budget.

Total hours	18,000	19,500	21,000
Forecast standard hours worked	17,000	17,000	17,000
Forecast overtime hours worked	1,000	2,500	4,000
Standard hours £	153,000	153,000	161,500
Overtime hours £		13,500	33,750
Labour cost for cash budget £	153,000	166,500	195,250

Other costs

Care should be taken with other costs, for example administration or distribution costs, as they may include a certain amount which relates to depreciation.

Depreciation is not a cash flow and therefore this amount should be excluded from the cash budget.

Exchange rates

A change in exchange rates might affect a business in the following ways:

- Exchange rate changes can increase or reduce the price of a product sold abroad.

- The price of imported raw materials may change.

- The price of competitors' products may change in the home market.

An exchange rate is the value of one currency expressed in terms of another. So, for example, £1 may be worth $1.50 in America and €1.39 in France.

Example

A business buys $4,000 of raw materials.

If the exchange rate is £1:$1.5000 then the sterling value of the raw materials is $4,000 ÷ 1.5000 = £2,667

If the exchange rate is $1:£0.6667 then the sterling value of the raw material is $4,000 × £0.6667 = £2,667

(rounded to the nearest whole £)

Interest

For cash budgeting purposes, the amount of interest will normally be calculated on the basis of the balance at the end of the month. The amount of interest to be received on a positive balance will be included in the following month's cash receipts and the amount of interest to be paid on a negative balance will be included in the following month's cash payments.

Example

The closing cash balance at the end of March is £4,500. Predicted cash inflows and outflows for April, May and June as are follows:

	April £	May £	June £
Receipt	42,155	93,785	96,535
Payments	−62,666	−105,347	−63,505

- 0.75% interest is received on a credit closing balance
- 2% interest is charged on a debit closing balance

Prepare the cash budget for April to June.

Cash budget for April to June

	April £	May £	June £
Receipts	42,155	93,785	96,535
Interest received	34*	0	0
Total receipts	42,189	93,785	96,535
Payments	−62,666	−105,347	−63,505
Overdraft interest	0	−320**	−557***
Total payments	−62,666	−105,667	64,062
Net cash flow	−20,477	−11,882	32,473

| Opening cash balance | 4,500 | −15,977 | −27,859 |
| Closing cash balance | −15,977 | −27,859 | 4,614 |

*4,500 × 0.75% = £34 (rounded to the nearest £)

** 15,977 × 2% = £320 (rounded to the nearest £)

*** 27,859 × 2% = £557 (rounded to the nearest £)

Loans

A business may take out a bank loan to be able to pay for new purchases. The receipt of the loan would be included in the receipts section of the cash budget. A loan will need to be paid back to the bank. There are 2 parts to a loan repayment – the capital (principal) repayment and the interest charged on the loan – these will both feature in the payments section of the cash budget.

Example

- A bank loan of £200,000 has been negotiated and this will be paid into the business bank account in October.

- The principal (capital) element of the bank loan is to be repaid in 50 equal monthly instalments beginning in November. Interest is to be paid at £800 per month for the first year, starting in November.

	Oct £	Nov £	Dec £
Receipts	403,910	641,740	743,290
Bank loan	200,000	0	0
Total receipts	603,910	641,740	743,290
Payments	−550,666	−755,347	−565,718
Bank loan capital repayment	0	−4,000	−4,000
Bank loan interest	0	−800	−800
Total payments	−550,666	−760,147	−570,518
Net cash flow	53,244	−118,407	172,772
Opening bank balance	4,500	57,744	−60,663
Closing bank balance	57,744	−60,663	112,109

4

Analysing and monitoring cash budgets

- Monitoring cash flows.
- Sensitivity analysis.
- Reconciliation of actual cash flow to budgeted cash flow.

Monitoring cash flows

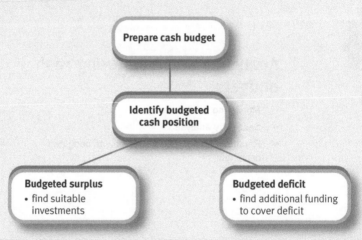

Prepare cash budget

Identify budgeted cash position

Budgeted surplus
• find suitable investments

Budgeted deficit
• find additional funding to cover deficit

CBA focus

In the exam you may be required to suggest what action should be taken if there is budgeted to be a surplus or a deficit.

Sensitivity analysis

What is the effect on the cash balance if cash receipts and/or cash payments change?

Example

Cash budget

	April	May	June
	£	£	£
Cash receipts	12,000	15,000	18,000
Cash payments	(10,000)	(14,000)	(24,000)
Net cash flow	2,000	1,000	(6,000)
Opening balance	4,000	6,000	7,000
Closing balance	6,000	7,000	1,000

By how much can the sales value for the three months fall before the business has to negotiate an overdraft?

Solution

If total sales value falls by £1,001 or more over the three month period then an overdraft will be required.

As a percentage of total sales this is a fall of £1,001/(12,000 + 15,000 + 18,000) x 100 = 2.22%

CBA focus

Discount offered to credit customers

- one way of using sensitivity analysis is to assess the effect on cash flows of offering a cash discount to credit customers for early payment.

Irrecoverable debts

- sensitivity analysis can also be used to assess the impact of credit customers failing to settle their debts.

Example

A business has the following budgeted credit sales and cash payments:

	April	May	June	July
	£000	£000	£000	£000
Credit sales	200	240	280	300
Cash payments	160	200	240	260

- 10% of credit customers pay in the month of sale
- remainder pay in the month after sale
- considering offering a 5% settlement discount for payment during the month of sale
- discount will be offered for sales from May onwards
- expected to result in 50% of customers taking advantage of the discount and the remainder still paying one month after the month of sale
- at the start of May there will be an overdraft of £20,000.

What is effect of offering cash discount on overall cash position?

Solution

Cash flows under existing policy

		April £000	May £000	June £000	July £000
Sales		200	240	280	300
April sales	(200 x 90%)		180		
May sales	(240 x 10%)		24		
	(240 x 90%)			216	
June sales	(280 x 10%)			28	
	(280 x 90%)				252
July sales	(300 x 10%)				30
Cash inflows			204	244	282
Cash outflows			(200)	(240)	(260)
Net cash inflow			4	4	22
Opening balance			(20)	(16)	(12)
Closing balance			(16)	(12)	10

Cash flows under proposed discount policy

		May £000	June £000	July £000
April sales	(200 x 90%)	180		
May sales	(240 x 50% x 95%)	114		
	(240 x 50%)		120	
June sales	(280 x 50% x 95%)		133	
	(280 x 50%)			140
July sales	(300 x 50% x 95%)			142.5
Cash inflows		294	253	282.5
Cash outflows		(200)	(240)	(260)
Net cash inflow		94	13	22.5
Opening balance		(20)	74	87
Closing balance		74	87	109.5

Under this new policy the overdraft is eliminated, although it must be appreciated that, in later periods, less cash will be received due to the discount.

CBA focus

In the exam, after preparing the cash budget, you may then be required to carry out some simple form of sensitivity or 'what if' analysis to determine the amended cash balance.

Reconciliation of actual cash flow to budgeted cash flow

- cash flow budgets are useful as part of the management process of control, where actual cash flows are compared to budgeted cash flows.

CBA focus

In the exam these reconciliations tend to take two forms:

- comparison of actual cash flows to budgeted cash flows
- reconciliation of budgeted cash balance to actual cash balance.

An understanding of the link between the budgeted and actual figures and the variances is needed as you may be required to work backwards to an actual or budget figure when given one of these and the variance.

Example

The actual and budgeted cash flows for the month of June were as follows:

	Actual £	Budget £
Receipts from receivables	67,700	71,200
Payments to payables	(38,900)	(37,200)
Wages and salaries	(13,200)	(13,800)
Expenses	(5,240)	(5,100)
Capital expenditure	(15,000)	–
Net cash flow	(4,640)	15,100
Opening cash balance	(10,000)	(10,000)
Closing cash balance	(14,640)	5,100

Identify the significant differences (more than a 4% difference) and suggest reasons for the differences between the actual cash flows and the budgeted cash flows.

Solution

Significant variances

Receipts are £3,500 less than budgeted, a 4.9% drop – customers may be delaying payment and/or sales receipts may be lower than forecast.

Payments are £1,700 more than budgeted, a 4.6% increase – purchases may be greater than forecast and/or payment may be being made quicker than budgeted.

Wages and salaries are £600 less than budgeted, a 4.3% drop – less hours may have been worked and/or forecast overtime may not have been required.

Capital expenditure has not been included in the budget at all. An unforeseen capital expense has been incurred or the budgeting was not accurate.

Note: expenses are not significant as the increase is only 2.7% above budget.

Example

Using the same data as per the previous example, reconcile the budgeted closing cash balance to the actual closing cash balance.

Solution

	£
Budgeted closing cash balance	5,100
Shortfall in receipts from receivables	(3,500)
Additional payments to payables	(1,700)
Lower wages and salaries	600
Additional expenses	(140)
Unbudgeted capital expenditure	(15,000)
Actual cash balance	(14,640)

After preparing a cash budget and possibly comparing it to actual figures you might then be asked to suggest what action might be taken if certain actual figures such as sales are falling behind the budgeted figures.

5

Liquidity management

- Liquidity.
- Working capital cycle.
- Measuring Liquidity.
- Gearing.
- Overtrading and over-capitalisation.

Liquidity

Definition

Liquidity is the measure of how much cash, liquid assets, or assets that are easily converted into cash, a business has.

Liquidity is a key contributing factor in the success or failure of a business.

Working capital cycle (or cash operating cycle)

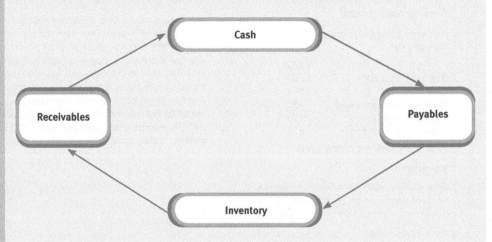

Calculating the working capital cycle

Inventory holding days + Receivable days – Payable days

e.g

Example

CBA focus

Working capital cycle

A business has the following figures for the last year:

	£000
Sales (all on credit)	1,200
Cost of sales	800
Receivables at year end	250
Payables at year end	180
Inventory at year end	220

What is the working capital cycle?

Solution

Inventory holding period = 220/800 x 365 = 100 days

Receivable collection period = 250/1,200 x 365 = 76 days

Payable payment period = 180/800 x 365 = (82 days)

Working capital cycle 94 days

If you were asked for the working capital cycle in months rather than days simply replace 365 in each calculation with 12 and the answer will appear in months. You may be asked to calculate one figure when provided with the working capital cycle total and two of the other figures. For example, calculate the receivable days when provided with the inventory and payable days and the working capital cycle total.

Measuring Liquidity

Return on capital employed = profit from operations ÷ capital employed × 100

Current ratio = current assets ÷ current liabilities

Quick ratio (acid test) = (current assets − inventory) ÷ current liabilities

Operating profit % = profit from operations ÷ revenue × 100

Return on shareholder' funds = profit after tax ÷ total equity × 100

Gearing

Gearing is a measure of the company's capital structure – is the business being funded by equity (repayable to shareholders) or by debt (repayable to banks).

If there is a lot of debt compared to the equity it is thought that a business is riskier as debt must be paid back to the banks when requested whereas equity does not have to be paid back to the shareholders on demand.

Gearing = total debt / (total debt + equity)

Total debt = All non-current liabilities ONLY

Overtrading and over-capitalisation

Overtrading
- inadequate cash to support the level of trading
- rapid sales growth
- increase in credit taken from credit suppliers
- fall in cash/increase in overdraft
- often increases in receivables/ inventories
- company must raise additional finance or slow down level of trading

Over-capitalisation
- too much long term finance
- loans should be repaid/shares repurchased

6

Raising finance

- The need to raise finance.
- Which one to choose?
- Bank overdraft.
- Bank loan.
- Debt factoring.
- Invoice discounting.
- Hire purchase.
- Leases.
- Sale and leaseback.
- Loan stock and debentures.
- Bonds.
- Crowdfunding.
- Equity shares.

The need to raise finance

There are many reasons why a business may need to raise additional finance, but the most common are:

- to fund working capital
- to purchase non-current assets
- to acquire another business.

Which one to choose?

Consideration should be made of:

- Cost – interest, fees, early redemption penalties
- Timescale – how long will the cash be required for
- Security – fixed and floating charges
- Impact on the gearing of the company

Interest rates

- Base interest rate – is the rate set by the Bank of England. Banks usually charge interest at 'an amount above base rate'.

- Fixed interest rate – an unchanging interest rate over the length of the period.

- Variable interest rate – the rate changes in line with an agreed indicator (usually in line with base interest rate but it can be another agreed index).

- Flat rate interest – is calculated based on the loan principal or capital amount. It is applied to the whole of the loan every year and does not take into account any repayments. The flat rate of interest can seem to be a lower option but in reality can be quite expensive.

- Simple interest – can be calculated by taking the total interest as a percentage of the original principal.

- Annual percentage rate (APR) – The

APR is an annual rate that is charged for borrowing (or made by investing), expressed as a single percentage number. It is calculated on the loan principal outstanding so that the interest charge reduces each monthly in line with the reduction in the amount outstanding. It represents the actual yearly cost of funds over the term of a loan. This includes any fees or additional costs associated with the transaction. This is the effective interest rate that a borrower will pay on a loan.

Security

- A fixed charge is where the security is a specific and identifiable asset or group of assets.
- A floating charge is where the security is supplied by a group of assets to the relevant value of the business such as receivables or inventory which will be constantly changing.

Bank overdraft

- Negotiated for a fixed period in terms of a maximum available facility.
- Take advantage of the facility as and when it needed.
- The interest will generally be at a variable rate, calculated on a day-to-day basis with reference to the bank's base rate.
- The business only pays interest on the amount actually drawn.
- Repayable on demand.

Effect on gearing and liquidity

Most calculations of gearing do not include the bank overdraft but if a company is being analysed for its potential credit worthiness it may be included. In CSFT, overdrafts are NOT included within total debt when calculating gearing.

The use of a bank overdraft is an indication that the business does not have enough cash to cover its commitments therefore may be having liquidity problems.

Bank loan

A term loan with a bank is a loan for a fixed amount, for an agreed period, on pre-arranged terms.

Term loans can be for virtually any period and the repayment terms can be negotiated with the bank:

- Interest rates may be fixed or variable.

Effect on gearing and liquidity

A bank loan would be included in the calculation of gearing and it will increase the level of gearing for a business as it is debt finance rather than equity finance.

The amount of loan recorded in the current liabilities will impact the liquidity ratio increasing the amount due versus the amount of current assets. This could have a bearing on the credit rating of a business.

Debt factoring

- Debt factoring is a continuing arrangement by which the factoring company purchases all the trade debts due to a business, as they arise.
- The business will be paid up to 80% of the value of invoices, with the balance coming on the date the invoice is settled, less a fee.
- The factoring may be with recourse or without recourse.
- The factoring company will generally take over responsibility for debt collection and sales ledger accounting.

Effect on gearing and liquidity

Gearing will not be affected by using a factor as there is no impact on the debt and equity of a business.

Factoring will improve short term liquidity as cash is advanced early by the factor. In the long term the company will receive less cash as the factor charges an administration fee and a finance fee.

Invoice discounting

Invoice discounting is another service provided by factoring companies.

Invoice discounting is simple and flexible, it can be used as and when short-term funds are needed and it enables the business to maintain a normal relationship with its customers.

Effect on gearing and liquidity

Gearing will not be affected by using an invoice discounter as there is no impact on the debt and equity of a business.

Invoice discounting will improve short term liquidity as cash is advanced early. In the long term the company has to repay the 'loan' plus interest so may have a bearing on long term liquidity.

Hire purchase

- If a non-current asset is to be purchased by the business, but there is not enough cash available for outright purchase, one simple method is to purchase the asset on a hire purchase scheme.

- Hire purchase and instalment credit arrangements can be set up quickly and can generally offer fairly flexible repayment terms.

- The security is provided by the asset being purchased.

- The main disadvantage of a hire purchase agreement is that the total payment for the asset can far outweigh actual purchase price.

Effect on gearing and liquidity

The balance of the loan in non-current liabilities is classed as long term debt and will therefore be included in the gearing calculation and may have a bearing on whether the business is able to raise more finance if needed.

The amount of hire purchase recorded in the current liabilities will impact the liquidity ratio increasing the amount due versus the amount current assets. This could have a bearing on the credit rating of a business.

Leases

A lease gives the lessee the right to use an asset in exchange for regular lease payments. This may be cheaper or easier than arranging finance to purchase the asset outright.

Accounting entries

With a standard lease the lessee will record the asset in the statement of financial position as if it is owned and will charge depreciation as normal.

A lease liability is also recognised (usually for the value of the asset) in non current liabilities.

The lease payments consist of an interest element and an element to pay off this liability.

The interest element is expensed as finance costs to the statement of profit or loss.

If it is a short term or low value item lease, no asset or liability is recognised and the lease payments are just treated as an expense in the statement of profit or loss.

Effect on gearing and liquidity

The gearing of the company will increase because the asset base increases but so does the total debt. The increase in gearing could affect the company's ability to raise additional finance. The liquidity of the business will not be affected by the acquisition but will be reduced by the lease payments.

Sale and leaseback

Sale and leaseback arrangements relate to property and large items of capital equipment. The company sells an asset to a financial institution which is then leased back to the company for a number of years.

Accounting entries

Sale of the asset i.e. a disposal:

- Step 1 – Remove the original cost of the disposed asset from the asset account
  Dr Disposals, Cr Non-current asset cost.

- Step 2 – Remove the accumulated depreciation of the disposed asset from the accumulated depreciation account
  Dr Non-current asset accumulated depreciation, Cr Disposals.

- Step 3 – Enter the sale proceeds received for the disposed asset
  Dr Bank, Cr Disposals.

- Step 4 – Balance off the ledger accounts and calculate whether a profit or loss has been made on disposal.

Lease repayments: as previously described.

Effect on gearing and liquidity

A sale and leaseback arrangement can provide an immediate source of cash, improving liquidity. The gearing will be increased by the lease liability. This may make it harder to obtain additional finance at a later date.

Loan stock and debentures

Any loan raised by the issue of a series of negotiable units could be described as 'loan stock'. Debenture describes the document which acknowledges the indebtedness.

Loan stock commonly has a fixed rate of interest.

They are repaid at a specified date.

Accounting entries

Debentures are not part of a company's share capital – they are third party liabilities. Debentures are shown as liabilities in the statement of financial position, just like any other loan.

Debenture interest is therefore a charge against profit and must be paid whether or not the company makes a profit.

Effect on gearing and liquidity

The debenture will increase the gearing of the company as it is increasing debt finance. The interest payments will have a bearing on the liquidity as current liabilities are increasing but also the cash from the loan will have increased current assets.

Bonds

Loans may be broken down into smaller units (e.g. one bond may have a nominal or par value of £100). Different varieties include debentures and loan stock and may be issued by companies, local authorities and governmental organisations.

Corporate bonds are used by many companies to raise funding for large-scale projects – such as business expansion, takeovers, new premises or product development.

The main features of a corporate bond are:

- the nominal value – the price at which the bonds are first sold on the market e.g. £1,000

- the interest (coupon) rate paid to the bond owner – this is usually fixed e.g. 5% the annual interest is the nominal value × coupon rate

- the redemption terms – when the nominal value of the bond must be repaid to the bond holder e.g. redeem at par in 2015.

Bonds can be sold on the open market to investment institutions or individual investors, or they can be sold privately.

Effect on gearing and liquidity

As the bond is effectively a loan it will increase the debt finance and therefore increase the gearing of a company.

The interest on the bond will have an impact on liquidity as it is recorded as a current liability and the cash received will be recorded as a current asset.

Crowdfunding

Particularly popular with small and start-up businesses, crowdfunding involves the use of an online platform (such as Kickstarter) to pitch their idea/product/business plan to a wide range of potential (usually small) investors. Crowdfunding can be used to raise either debt or equity.

As well as raising new finance, it can also help boost brand awareness and help build a customer base.

Effect on gearing and liquidity

The impact on gearing will depend on in crowdfunding is used to raise equity (which will decrease gearing) or debt (which will increase gearing).

The finance raised will boost cash and hence liquidity levels but if debt is raised then the additional liabilities may reduce the possibilities of raising further debt in the future.

Equity Shares

Companies issue shares to raise capital, usually in the form of cash although shares may be issued in exchange for assets.

The term equity relates to ordinary shares only. Equity finance is the investment in a company by the ordinary shareholders, represented by the issued ordinary share capital plus reserves.

Effect on gearing and liquidity

Issuing shares should have a positive effect on gearing as it increases the equity finance of a company.

Cash levels are increased when shares are issued so this will have a positive effect on liquidity of a company.

7

Investing surplus funds

- General requirements for investing.
- Types of investment.

General requirements for investing

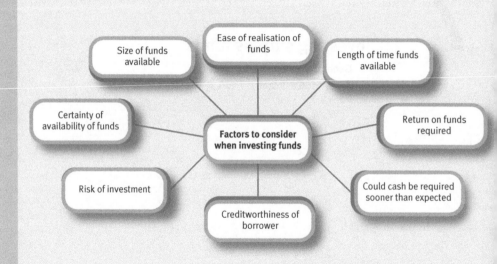

Size of funds available

Ease of realisation of funds

Length of time funds available

Certainty of availability of funds

Factors to consider when investing funds

Return on funds required

Risk of investment

Creditworthiness of borrower

Could cash be required sooner than expected

Key factors

Risk

- Risk that value of investment will fall.
- Risk that return from investment will be lower than expected.

Return

- Generally the higher the risk of the investment the higher the return.
- Ease of realisability of investment often reflected in return.

Liquidity

- Often penalties for early realisation of investment so cash availability must be certain.

CBA focus

It is important that you understand these key factors in making investments as you may need to discuss these as a basis for choosing investments in an assessment.

Types of investment

Certificates of deposit (CDs)
- negotiable instruments issued by a bank
- usually minimum of £50,000
- can be traded or held to maturity
- highly marketable therefore very liquid

Bank/building society deposit accounts
- variety of types of account
- interest rates will vary according to terms/notice period

Types of investment

Treasury bills
- issued by Bank of England on behalf of Government
- sold at discount and repaid at face value at end of issue period

Local authority bills
- issued by individual local authorities
- less active market than gilts/Treasury bills so less liquid and higher return

Government securities
- known as gilt-edged securities
- fixed interest
- very low risk
- highly marketable

Commodities
- an economic good or service when the demand for it has no qualitative differentiation across a market
- for example a barrel of oil is basically the same product, regardless of the producer
- Commodities come into and go out of fashion over time. Supply and demand for commodities can change liquidity

Corporate bonds
- issued by a company
- high risk as the price will fluctuate
- higher return
- Long term

Types of investment

Land and property
- historically deemed to be a fairly safe investment
- can only be realised once the land or property is sold
- any initial investment may not be fully realised if there has been a drop in market value
- long term investment

Shares
- shares are considered to be the most risky of investment opportunities
- the return possible from shares is higher than that of the other options
- shares can be bought and sold

8

Impact of regulations and policies on financing and investment

- Government and the Bank of England.
- The Bank of England.
- Investment regulations.
- Economic factors.
- Ethical considerations.

The Government and the Bank of England

The Government can affect an organisation's treasury function by controlling the supply of money, interest rates and the availability of credit.

Governments have two main ways of affecting the economy:

Fiscal policy refers to the government's taxation and spending plans.

Monetary policy refers to the management of the money supply (the total amount of money, including currency in circulation and deposited in banks and building societies) in the economy.

The Bank of England and the treasury function

The Bank of England has control over interest rates, which will influence what an organisations treasury function will wish to do with any surplus funds.

When interest rates are low:

- Money is less expensive to borrow so people will spend more.
- This can create employment opportunities and expansion within businesses that require capital investment.
- It will also create inflation.

When interest rates are high:

- Money is more expensive to borrow which leads to higher levels of saving or investing.
- The government will attempt to reduce inflation rates to try to encourage people to spend money.

Quantitative easing

A relatively unconventional monetary policy
that involves the Bank of England buying
financial assets (such as government and
corporate bonds) using money that it has
generated electronically. The bank has
essentially printed itself new money that it
can spend.

The Bank of England

Maintain integrity/ value currency
- inflation targets lead to setting of short term interest rates monthly

Maintain stability of financial system
- monitors developments in financial system in UK and abroad

Core purpose of Bank of England

Promote effectiveness of UK's financial services
- monitors competitive threats to City of London and other centres of financial services

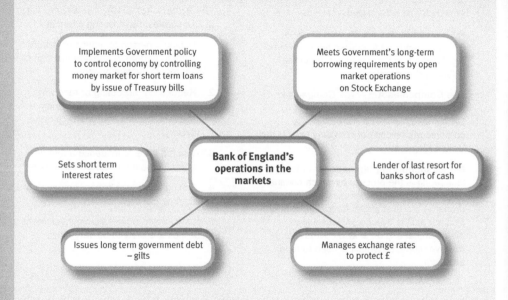

Investment regulations

Private companies are allowed to invest their own funds as they wish but there are regulations to adhere with set out in the following documents:

The Companies Act – The Companies Act 2006 forms the primary source of UK company law. The Act provides a comprehensive code of company law for the United Kingdom.

Money laundering regulations – Money laundering is the process by which criminally obtained money or other assets (criminal property) are exchanged for 'clean' money or other assets with no obvious link to their criminal origins. It also covers money, however come by, which is used to fund terrorism.

The Bribery Act 2010 – The Bribery Act (2010) creates the following offences:

1 Bribing a person to induce or reward them to perform a relevant function improperly (active bribery).

2 Requesting, accepting or receiving a bribe as a reward for performing a relevant function improperly (passive bribery).

3 Using a bribe to influence a foreign official to gain a business advantage.

4 Failing to prevent bribery on behalf of a commercial organisation.

In public sector organisations, investment guidelines are likely to be very strict.

Economic factors

Local vs global economies

Expanding in the local economy is likely to be easier for a business to achieve as it will have already established a brand presence and will have greater awareness of competitors and customers' needs. However expanding overseas in the global economy can open up much larger potential markets and allow the business to grow much larger and at a faster rate.

Exchange rates

When buying or selling goods in a foreign currency, changes in the exchange rate can either help or hinder the business.

For a UK company, a strengthening of the UK pound (e.g. the exchange rate moving from $1.45:£1 to $1.50:£1) will make overseas purchases cheaper, but reduce the sterling value of overseas sales.

Organisational policies

If the economy is healthy and growing well it will be easier for a business to raise finance and find new opportunities to expand, however if the economy is in a recession then finance is likely to be harder to obtain, and a business is more likely to choose more liquid investments for any surplus cash in case the money is required at short notice.

Ethical considerations

Ethical issues must also be considered when a business is investing in new projects or in other businesses.

If an organisation is using or investing in a less than reputable company this could have a serious negative impact on how the organisation is perceived by customers, suppliers and employees.

Index

KAPLAN PUBLISHING